T0368382

Master *Of* Fabrication

Why create a life that isn't made for you?

Hadeel

authorHOUSE®

AuthorHouse™ UK
1663 Liberty Drive
Bloomington, IN 47403 USA
www.authorhouse.co.uk
Phone: UK TFN: 0800 0148641 (Toll Free inside the UK)
UK Local: (02) 0369 56322 (+44 20 3695 6322 from outside the UK)

Published by AuthorHouse 10/30/2024

ISBN: 979-8-8230-9019-3 (sc)
ISBN: 979-8-8230-9020-9 (hc)
ISBN: 979-8-8230-9024-7 (e)

Library of Congress Control Number: 2024921510

Print information available on the last page.

Any people depicted in stock imagery provided by Getty Images are models, and such images are being used for illustrative purposes only. Certain stock imagery © Getty Images.

This book is printed on acid-free paper.

Because of the dynamic nature of the Internet, any web addresses or links contained in this book may have changed since publication and may no longer be valid. The views expressed in this work are solely those of the author and do not necessarily reflect the views of the publisher, and the publisher hereby disclaims any responsibility for them.

CHAPTER 1

....

My time so far at Detroit has been quite miserable and lonely I had no one to talk to but my friend back home and one best friend who was close to me since she was in Texas. I had just comeback from my walk and surprisingly my internet was working so I managed to catch my friends call and she asked me how my holiday was going so far? I could not lie at least to her I can be honest because even if she knew the cold hard truth it's not like anything can be done to make the situation better as unfair that was to my family I just could not tell them the truth at least not yet. When I started to divulge into the recent issues happening my friend couldn't believe what was being said because it truly is hard to trust anyone word without any evidence or witnessing it right before your eyes but since she knew me very well to know what accusations Lei may have said is not true which did feel nice. Shortly after Lei heard me laughing and came rushing to the kitchen asked me who are you speaking with? Is that a boy voice I hear? I immediately told her NOOO it's not just because she is sick and has a raspy voice doesn't automatically make her a boy and I even showed her my phone since my friend has a picture in her profile to prove even further that it isn't a boy however I shouldn't even have proven who I'm speaking with. I am free to speak whoever I wanted but Lei wanted and prayed I had spoken with a boy so she can report back to my family and Harry that it is the reason I'm getting sleepless nights and not eating right because I'm speaking with a boy. The real reason behind me not eating good and not sleeping because the noises I hear at night is absolutely horrifying and I bet no human being can sleep to it no matter how tired they are it is incredibly hard. I would hear constant moans and by each hour it becomes even louder to the point I'd hear some breakage as if there was somebody else in the room with Lei now for those reading must be thinking well it could've been Harry with her in the bedroom as a matter of a fact Harry was never in Detroit never in the house and never around his wife as how close they made it seem before I had even came to Detroit he just never wished or wanted to be in the house and anytime I asked why don't you stay a bit longer his excuse was always work which I'd like to believe but you just got married wouldn't you want to go places with your wife or even take her out to restaurants. Before I came we had this amazing plan to go outside Detroit such a beaches, amusements parks and vintage stores as well as paintballing but we never got to any of the stuff we had planned because anytime Harry would say you ready for an epic day and his wife would say no we aren't going to those horrid dangerous places what if she got hurt or worse died and Harry responded with yeah you're probably right I don't want to be in trouble with her mother later on. His response sounded as if he was possessed and not thinking for himself her words echoed through him, he did not even act like the person I knew before sad to say. From the first day on the day we were picked up from the airport for years countless summers Harry and William and grandmother would always be the people me and my family witness at the airport when they come to pick us but I saw Mary coming rushing to me and grandmother I ask her who is that she says oh well darling that's Lei I told her she looks quite terrifying and asked well where is both Harry and William she said William is at work but may swing by home later on and Harry is at the car waiting. It sounded all odd to me no matter how hectic their schedules they always are here for us but ever since Lei joined the herd it all came crashing down. At around this time I was already a week into Detroit and felt quite drained and upset because I had no one to talk with and listen to me talk about what's really going on. Nobody seemed to believe me not even my friend she thought it was all a lie especially since she spoke briefly with Lei and thought that someone with her light sweet voice it would be impossible for her to do what I claim she had done. It felt as if the entire world was against me and that I was in a board game and knew no rules on how to navigate but be shoved in a place where no one was on my side, I was too afraid to talk with my parents because I know for sure they would go confront Harry which I didn't want to happen just because it would cause some issues and I would most likely be asked to elaborate when I had no evidence to back up my story which would evidentially make me seem like a liar. When I would walk around just for daily exercise steps or when I would go to the stores I usually felt quite happy but after witnessing Lei horrible moments and how she treated me for no reason everything seemed grey I personally didn't wish to do anything but wait my days out till I can go back to my family.

CHAPTER 2

....

I'll be talking about how I felt abandoned and disposed by my family how I wished to talk about what was making me upset nobody wanted to hear me out. When they asked me, I tried telling them but they just dismissed my feelings and didn't take me seriously when I told them what I saw. One day my grandmother requested me walk after Lei little meltdown and I told her seriously look at me and tell me that you don't see how she acts and treats you she told me 'I do see but if you love Harry you wouldn't cause any problems and keep quiet about what you see and just enjoy your remaining days' I was completely shocked by her reply and didn't know what to tell her so I did what she asked me but it utterly gutted me. I knew my grandmother was extremely reserved didn't want to discuss her issues with anyone not even with her siblings because of what others would think of her and may judge on her actions however, asking your guest your own blood the person you took well care of when we would visit you to just shut up and take whatever comes your way just to make Lei happy and not disrupt Harry whilst he driving on the expense of your nieces happiness and mental health. I was pretty much a prisoner in the house not allowed to go outside myself, not allowed to speak or express my concerns and not even allowed to speak with my friends or family in case I said something by mistake or broke down but no it never occurred to them that it may affect me long time only to make Lei happy. I wasn't even allowed to cry or show any signs of sadness only time I got to let it out just so I don't explode in front of them was solely in my room and it kept me up all night only time I heard a decent human being was at 4:45am when I would call my mother and hear a true genuine loving voice but even then I couldn't even express my feelings. After hearing what my grandmother wanted from me I felt like I had no right to tell my mother what was making me upset she knew deep down that something wasn't right but waited till I told her I couldn't betray my grandmother or Harry even after what I saw I still loved them. After my call with mother ended I collapsed because I was so tired I just couldn't stay up anymore I had a missed call from Harry so I called him as soon as I woke up and he said ' Wassup dude how are you?' it did feel like he cared but as long as he was connected to Lei it just didn't seem like the same just wasn't sincere. I told him yes, I'm okay are you? How is your travel so far? My grandmother had called me for dinner to join her and Lei, Harry thought she was yelling at me and said hold on love I'm going to be back he proceed to call grandmother and asked why are you yelling at your niece be a little calmer and gentler when you speak with her she is our family after hearing that it felt like there was hope and that perhaps I haven't lost them at all I did feel a little happier than the previous night. Grandmother came into my room and said I didn't yell at you I only asked for you to join us I hope you didn't see it as me screaming at you I'm sorry love. Whilst grandmother was apologising to me I can hear Lei from the dining hall yelling and she meant it for sure and said ' IF YOU GUYS AREN'T COMING TO EAT IM GOING TO AND I DON'T CARE IF YOU EAT OR NOT' I thought to myself should you really even be saying that your mother in law I just thought it was incredibly rude and disgusting how she speaks to my grandmother I told Lei we're coming and even if we didn't eat with you go right ahead I honestly don't want to eat with you I lose my appetite quickly she then leaves the dining hall and goes to call Harry. Grandmother told me it was okay you didn't need to stick up for me I looked confused as to why my grandmother didn't want me saying anything yes I knew she didn't want any issues but it wasn't correct what Lei said of course I had to stand up for my grandmother after all I didn't and never will consider Lei as my family. Shortly after Harry called me and said 'How dare you speak to my beloved wife like that??' You really don't deserve for anyone to care about you I can't believe I even asked from you to take care of Lei when you can't even be nice to her and I replied with she's the one who's talking rudely to your mother your own mother who she sacrificed a lot and you even said yourself she is a red line no one crosses her but yet you let this new women speak ill of her it just made no sense to me. Her told me she is my wife so if my mother did something bad Lei has the right to educate her, and I was confused by educate her seemed like Lei was the one lacking life skills not the other way round. Just seemed like he had forgotten who his priority is yes, his wife may be someone important to him but it doesn't mean she can speak poorly to grandmother. A guy had contacted Harry about Lei saying that she was first engaged to me and that this women isn't who you think she is because I met her through a game and I had spent a fortune on her and her family only to be played like a fool and went to get married to you now. Either you ask Lei to return the money to me and apologise for playing me like a fool or atleast some sort of explanation as this isn't appropriate for a women like her especially since I thought she was raised right from such a proper family or so he thought. Harry was so angry at the time he couldn't think rationally and just got mad at everyone but first he blocked this mysterious guy and then confronted Lei knowing this women she's going to lie 100%. Obviously that's what she did because she's still here today all safe and not harmed at all she practically got down on her knees started to rub her hands together pleading to Harry claiming all these accusations came from nowhere and is actually relating to another women and not her she has no idea why this man is speaking ill of her. Harry believed Lei for the moment till he went to work later that evening and then he got a mysterious text from THAT SAME MAN, saying ' How dare you block me?!?' Fine you want to play that game let me send you pictures and screenshots it was so much and a lot of proof that Harry called William saying what should he do? And William said well you should talk to your wife why call me and ask what to do this is a private matter that should be spoken of quickly as its very damaging to us as well go fix it. Harry calls Lei and says get ready pack your bags you're going home…! Rather than fix the issue Harry just wanted to fly Lei out to her family which I would've loved a lot at the time but of course as soon as he got home he thought she had left but instead she was sitting on the kitchen dinning table with grandmother drinking tea so of course Harry was fuming said WHAT ARE YOU STILL DOING HERE? Grandmother has no idea so she yells at Harry saying this isn't how you should treat your wife I'm quite glad I'm still in this house of what would've you done to this poor girl huh. Harry said well she isn't that innocent now whilst Harry explains to grandmother Lei did the same thing she did when she was let off with this issue by getting down on her knees and begging for forgiveness from the both of them. Harry says GET OFF THE FLOOR AND DON'T COME NEAR ME WHO ARE YOU? They didn't speak for sometime but afterwards the mysterious man calls Harry and said it's all a mistake I'm sorry I didn't mean to send you all this nonsense. Now that's so weird to me because the other day he was adamant that it was Lei and now he said wrong girl I'm so confused! .Firstly Lei had lied about her identity completely felt like it was straight out of a movie I've never seen/met or come across anyone who is willing to lie like that and that she had all these amazing skills turns out she is nothing but a problematic women who only wanted to wreak havoc and that is simply what she had done. Everyone in the house was suspicious of each other didn't want to eat any left overs and what was the worst part is her accusing those in the house of her having a serious issue with her lady parts and that she could've contracted from the toilet seat which was stupid pardon my language but I laughed at the time it was absolutely ridiculous I couldn't contain my laughter only then she started to point fingers at me and looked at Harry whilst her eyes was filled with tears and said LOOK look at your niece she is trying to sabotage our only chance at having a child what are you going to do are you going to punish her this isn't fair. Uncle Harry just yelled at me and said I never want to see you all you've done with your time here is cause issues and not help my wife nor my mother. It seemed to me that nobody wanted me and wished that I was anywhere but at their house. For many years my grandmother's house felt like a second home someone I can rely on as well as Harry they were there for me and my siblings but it didn't seem like that my last holiday with them. William wife Beth asked me if I wanted to join them on William birthday and I thought it was an amazing idea of course I wanted to go actually to be completely honest I would've done anything to leave the house just because I felt suffocated at home. Beth told me great I will be at grandmother's house at around 2pm on 1st July and we shall go collect the cake and go meet up with your William at work to go together for the restaurant. Lei had overheard my conversation with Beth and said you absolutely won't be able to go it's also your grandmother and Harry birthday how could you abandon them on their birthday firstly I already felt abandoned by them I mean it was totally unfair of her to even ask that, but my great grandmother had passed away not too long ago it was the real reason why my grandmother was in London in the first place and why I went back with her to her hell hole house she claims to be loving. Grandmother heard yelling and came running from the garden where she was attending to the vegetable garden and said why are you guys yelling I told her I'm not Lei came in out of nowhere and forbid me from going out with Beth and William celebrating his birthday.

Before I go deeper into why I was forbidden from going out with William and Beth is because Lei has such deep deep hatred for Beth and her daughter she doesn't love them and doesn't wish them well. Prior to my arrival Lei had caused quite a lot of drama for Beth to the point where she requested Harry pick her or his brother and sister in law he automatically said he will pick them anyway before her just because it was before they got married and hadn't known her for long and even cared for her. Which does make me wonder how he is so infatuated with Lei he also said the one thing most people would break off a wedding much less marriage by him saying I don't even love her and she even knew that he said that so why on this green earth did Lei even go through with everything. I'll tell you why she was in trouble with another guy whom she met on pubG which is a computer game and got so serious with him he started to develop feelings for and wished to marry her he even proposed to Lei and she accepted only so he would send her money which he did that amounted to $6000 after that Lei didn't ever talk with him, no facetime, or calls nothing it's as if she used him for money practically toyed with his feelings for a load of money. When my grandmother was rushed to the hospital because she hadn't been eating and felt quite oozy she didn't seem like her usual self and I was very concerned for her and told her I'll happily order an uber to take you to the hospital and can accompany you. Lei and Harry said no you'll not go because you have asthma and it'll get worse since covid was still alive and making people sick which felt odd since it was the first time I had the seen 'the couple' worried about me I was adamant about going with grandmother mostly because I didn't trust Lei to be alone with her since she is an evil incarnate. So Harry advised Lei to stay with me and he will go with grandmother to the hospital and will try to make it back just before evening, I was terrified enough this women slept just a few feet away from me at night and now I have to spend my morning with her not to mention it was hailing outside not like I could go and stroll around till it was evening. But then again I thought to myself I come from London it is raining about almost everyday when wasn't it raining and it is just water so I wasn't really bothered by it so once my grandmother and Harry walked outside and got into the car drove off I wore my coat as soon as possible and ran straight for the door until Lei came rushing and said where are you going??? I said well I'm going out don't particularly feel like staying in the house since grandmother isn't too well I can't just sit idly and wish to grab some fresh air. Lei yelled at me saying well it's raining it is extremely unsafe for you to walk outside I said like you just mentioned it's just raining nothing serious I'll be fine, till she suggested well I'm coming with you oh man did I wish she slipped and layed in the couch I seriously didn't want her to come along and I said if anything happens to you it's not my problem you're forcing yourself to come with me. Lei responded with you should take care of me I told her I'm younger by you than a decade who should be taking care of who and besides I wouldn't trust you with a pencil much less my life. She was very angry which isn't my main concern right now since I had other stuff on my mind we walked halfway to Starbucks which was about a good 15minutes walk and she was completely drenched best thing to ever happen to her without me having to do anything. Lei shouted 'HERE IS STARBUCKS GO IN AND GET YOUR COFFEE AND LETS GO' I said I wasn't planning on going there and she said well where were you going, I replied with its really none of your business if you wish to go back home you're more than free to do so I can go back home myself I know the way and the rain will clear up in a few don't need you around. She warned me by saying if you don't come along right now and get coffee and walk back home I'll call Harry and say why you aren't coming back home told her that's fine go right ahead doesn't bother me I'll just say how you forced yourself to come with me when you weren't invited. Lei looks at me speechless and starts to walk to the door of Starbucks whilst I cross the road to Target and Panera Bread I heard they have really good tomato soup with strawberry lemon iced tea which are both my favourite and because it just felt very nice to sit and eat soup with a cold beverage whilst admiring the rain and just casually walk to Target get whatever I need to survive the next upcoming days with Lei the devil. When I say grab what I need to survive mostly its coffee or strong coffee mix for me to stay up so I wouldn't be bothered by Lei as she has a tendency to just walk into my room with no warning at all why that is a question only god can answer himself. She'd come in and ask very random very idiotic questions mind my manners but they were extremely ridiculous I couldn't even hold my laughter most of the time but it was super consistent I just got tired of answering or even hearing her voice.

There was a point where I just wanted to be alone I got so tired of everyone just assuming I was alright and thinking that Lei was some sort of angel that came down to Amboy street to make everything and everyone happy as if we weren't already only got worse when she got here. At times I felt unheard which would be quite normal in most cases had the person I spoke to was tired or depressed yet nobody in the house seemed like that because they were always checking if Lei was okay and if she needed anything but not the guest oh no! I had to keep my feelings in check and if I felt any anger it had to go because I wasn't allowed to feel that way or even try and express my concerns. Harry asked me if I was truly okay and that if I didn't we would go to Starbucks when he was back and tell him what was bothering me because he knew deep down that anytime we would go to Detroit we were always so happy and never felt any bit of sadness. I was really happy that he said will go talk just the two of us because I really wanted alone time with Harry for me to explain everything that Lei has been doing. Harry was extremely confused about what Lei has been doing and saying towards me and grandmother, because he really believes Lei is innocent and only wishes the best for us which is the complete opposite of her actions. I didn't always hate Lei I actually loved her and that was before I went up to Detroit she seemed like this sweet innocent lady who only wished the best for those around her. I honestly thought she loved me and was dying to meet me till it came with requests and attachments such as me getting her multiple gifts, teaching her English, getting her a remote job I didn't mind at all I thought it was a reasonable request because I cared for her and only wanted to help her since she wanted to make herself better which I admired. But once I got to Detroit she didn't want to learn English no more but still dream of getting a good job with a reasonable pay even though she had no CV, no experience and only wished to work a few days a week for at least 2hrs a day which was absolutely insane and crazy demands considering she had nothing to offer I truly was confused and anytime I would filter out the jobs that were available she didn't like it and wanted me to negotiate with the recruiting manager. Whilst I was speaking to her soon to be manager Lei took my phone because Harry had called me to check up as usual when he is off to work. However, I had received multiple messages from me which was super weird because firstly I had Lei blocked and moved to archive meaning she must've unblocked herself. I really shouldn't have opened the messages but I was curious as to why she was going through my phone when she was only meant to answer Harry and see how he is, so when I checked the texts it was screenshots of my chat with Harry nothing special just funny memes or gifs and I thought is she that jealous and desperate to know what goes on with Harry and William I mean I knew she has this fiery pit in her heart when I talk and laugh with Harry and her not knowing what's going on but it's gotten quite silly and ridiculous for her to pry on my messages. So I thought to myself since she wants to secretly take her time checking out and seeing if there is any trouble with my messages to make her rage even more I deleted the messages from my side since I had her phone for the interview I had taken so much time to help her when she's not even grateful. I gave her phone back and she went into her room thinking I'm stupid enough to not see a message from someone who clearly has full knowledge that I blocked her in the first place. She comes out of her room yelling and screaming saying ' I'm going to be divorced all because of your stupid granddaughter what are you going to do about her she's such a problematic person' I had tried to console with my grandmother get to her first and tell her what she did all my grandmother said so what it's her husband let her do whatever she wants so I said its okay for her to take everyone's phone whom Harry is in contact with and secretly take screenshots and send to herself. That is not right and clearly someone should speak with her I mean the least she could do is ask I mean it's not like there is anything for her to see. Shortly after my mother calls and hears all the commotion asked me who's yelling like a crazy person I tell her sadly its Lei my mother at this point has no clue what Lei has done and hurt me because I've kept her in the dark which I do realize was the wrong thing to do but anyways my grandmother runs after Lei as she said I'm packing to go back home and never returning at this point grandmother is scared because she grabbed her suitcases and was starting to throw clothes into her bag as if we actually cared wait let me rephrase I didn't care since I was the only one who knew the truth. I accidentally forgot my mother was on call with me and I said thank god she's going who wants her and my mother replies back with what do you mean what has she been doing why don't you want her to stay or at least convince her that we want her I said well mother I will explain everything when I get back that's when I thought no problems would blow up or well get any worse than it is now I was mistaken. Anyways grandmother ran to Lei room and Lei I swear to god has no respect for her elders and doesn't care if grandmother got hurt quite literally slammed the door onto grandmothers foot and she said OW! Lei you're hurting me looks down as if she was the one who got hurt I looked quite confused and said to myself who should be the one who's in excruciating pain right now is it Lei or my grandmother. Lei left the door because she wanted to close the door shut and god knows what feed false information to Harry, grandmother went inside the room and talked to Lei down as if it would've worked that's when grandmother started to yell herself and say what a crazy wife in law oh my god jeez who do we have here has no respect for nobody and only wants what she wishes. At that exact moment I had stars in my eyes I felt like I was finally being heard nope, I wasn't because my grandmother came outside and said look what you've done I can't believe you deleted those photos should've just let her see it if there is nothing wrong with them but I said she should've asked and secondly I had her blocked meaning she was looking for our conversation like we had any ha-ha! Then Lei turns it back on and said well why did you have me blocked and I flat out said well darling frankly you're quite annoying and I can't believe someone was stupid enough to marry and women like you who has no personality and attitude is so horrible it still blows my mind that people actually like you. Once I said that she immediately cried and my grandmother yelled at me she had never yelled sometimes it was just a joke to get me to do something but this time I truly felt hated and grandmother said I don't ever want to see you until you go off back home I can't believe I've brought you with me. That's when I called mother but held my tears back and told mother what grandmother said because I still had about 2 weeks to go I was about to erupt and the bad thing still hadn't happened yet so when I said that grandmother wished she didn't bring me here mother said oh well that's odd she didn't even pay for the ticket why on earth would she say that when I told her about what Lei did mother said don't worry I'm going to call Harry and straighten his wife out at that moment I knew nothing was going to change but it was worth a shot. Harry then calls me and said I'm sorry love I didn't think Lei would've done this but you shouldn't have deleted the photos so it seems that this is normal when people screenshot photos and send to themselves what era, generation are we living in where it's okay to take screenshots or other peoples conversation.

On 13th July 2022 Harry asked me lets go get coffee just the two of us on this day I didn't realise it would've been the end of my friendship with Harry. Lei said well I'm coming with the both of you why should you two have fun and I stay at home with grandmother just cleaning, cooking and protecting a house with nobody to actually entertain. I looked at Uncle Harry and thought to myself did your wife actually just say those words or am I dreaming because that is incredibly rude not only to Harry and to grandmother the women who took this poor orphan into our beloved home. I said no thank you Harry I can walk to Tim Hortons by myself and I feel like I haven't walked very long and my legs are quite tired I need to exercise get my daily steps I didn't actually mean it not like I have been eating very well to go out long it would just tire me out and I have this invisible battle with Lei. Most of the time when I'd be alone with Lei she would try and do her absolute best to make me hate William and Beth because it seemed she had issues with them before I came along and had I hated them like Lei wished then it would give her evidence to Harry that they're in fact bothering Lei since she arrived in Detroit. I only ever gave Lei the truth about how I truly think of Beth and William and I love them always and forever as I have never doubted myself and they have always been by myside and supported me compared to grandmother and Harry throughout this holiday I hadn't received so much as a thank you or a like of love. Felt as if their love for me since the day I was born had completely taken a 360 turn onto Lei and pushed me into the darkness like I didn't matter to them or the fact that I was a guest in their house which they always say my house is yours didn't feel like that quite the opposite like I was pushed off the property but at the same time to show my mother that I was still there and wanted but that wasn't the truth. I'd wake up really early where the time in London would be 7am and I'll call my mother she'd ask me why I woke up super early since no one else is up and that I'm on holiday I should be resting however, due to the inconvenience of Lei disturbance I couldn't sleep not that I could tell my grandmother or Lei that she is quite literally more annoying than the constant planes coming in the USA and out. However, I didn't see any reason to bother my mother and tell her why I was up but simply say I missed her and wanted to hear her voice I didn't think she bought what I said but it moved things along till she wanted to see the house and garden that's when it got a little nasty because Lei had woken up and took my phone because she wanted to speak with mother non other than why I'm not eating her food and not going out. As always Lei wished to cause issues for me

I just said I simply wasn't energetic to go out with her I did feel incredibly upset with myself because I couldn't bring myself to tell mother the truth why I couldn't go out with Lei since I didn't come up with a good reason why mother puppy eyed me quite literally guilt me into going out with Lei at the time we were shopping in Target I truly felt like she would leave me to pay everything and run off and when I say run off I mean drive off without me back home not that Target is far but with all the ridiculous amount of stuff she is putting in the cart it would be almost impossible for me to pick it all up and take with me back home. Shortly after walking through aisle 12 Lei holds her stomach falls onto the cart holding it tightly mentioning she needs to use the bathroom and quickly rushed to the exit where the bathroom is located. I just stood and continued to shop because I asked her if she wanted me to go with her as Uncle Harry said whilst I'm on the job you must take care of her so I asked and she simply said no continue to shop whilst rushing as her voice echoed through the aisles. I called mother as I saw it my opportunity to ask her and my siblings what they wanted from the states obviously wouldn't do it near Lei as she would just charge it on Uncle Harry card and he works too hard besides I can't let her do it to him I know he wouldn't mind there's just no need for it. My mother said to bring some candy for my siblings and coffee had I found the brand there as you see we are huge Tim Hortons fan we absolutely adore Tim Horton we think it is the best coffee out there the essence of the coffee beans is unlike any other I have ever had especially the medium roast truly heaven like. It's been half an hour I still haven't seen any signs of Lei so I wondered to myself did she leave me I know we have our bickering but surely she didn't just leave me and lie about her stomach however, I wouldn't put it past her even my mother asked who did I come with so I said well Lei gave me a ride well actually she begged me but I couldn't exactly tell her just yet that Uncle Harry begged me to take care of his wife. So I said Lei rushed to bathroom because her stomach supposedly hurt her but I haven't heard of her I mean she could send a message not that she was my first priority. My mother left but said to take care of myself and that she'll call grandmother it didn't feel too good with me but oh well not that I did anything perhaps Lei true colours would show and may all be well in this travel. When I went to check out well before I did just in case Lei had actually left me I put all her stuff back because it was very heavy no way I could pick it up by myself so I paid and went outside only to be horribly correct she had actually left me so whilst I started to make my journey back by foot which was the best no one near me to pester me about anything or put their nose where it surely shouldn't be. Uncle Harry called me I thought it was just for him to check on Lei but no he called to lecture me as to why I didn't run after Lei and check to her wounds I said she didn't trip to have a wound it's just her stomach probably a stomach bug or she caught the flu nothing major really and said well get home then we will discuss this when I get home how you should really take care of Lei when I'm not there. He didn't even ask me how I would get home or if I needed help I mean what a lovely Uncle really truly I mean he was never like this. Anyways it took me about 30 minutes to get home it could've took me less but I had an urge for Starbucks I just couldn't resist it was right in front of me quite literally pulling me in to order. I ended up with iced caramel macchiato with 3 extra double shots not good for my health but it surely gives me a caffeine buzz which is exactly what I needed if Lei intended to be around. Grandmother lectured me why I didn't leave the groceries and attend to Lei I said she left me and ran to bathroom was I to go after her??? After she clearly said continue with the shopping she clearly gave me her clear instructions but grandmother urged me that what I had done was wrong and Lei was first priority. After Lei comes crawling from the corridor and said well where is the stuff I put in the cart I said I put it back because you left surely you didn't expect me to carry it all after you left quite hilarious of you to think so. She screamed so loud that the entire neighbourhood heard quite literally our next door neighbour came by and asked what was that noise is everything okay grandmother didn't even tell her the truth and said something fell yes because when an object falls to the floor it sounds like a human scream. I was really confused why grandmother didn't tell her friend the truth not only are they our neighbour but grandmothers friend obviously she didn't believe what was told to her but couldn't claim my grandmother lied to her either. Lei this time didn't leave so quickly she actually stayed till I gave her a good reason and I just told her the truth I think by in this trip it was the only thing I actually said that was truthful without having to be cautious of anyone's feelings or if I said anything it'll cause issues but her Lei hearing this brought me great joy! I simply said you left me to attend to your ' wounds' there is no way I could possibly carry everything so I just left them on the side it's not like the things you had put in the cart were exclusive, limited edition they could easily be obtained anyway so don't worry love it's okay. I had to be careful with what I say otherwise it'll sound like I did this all purposely when it's just a coincidence and I saw my shot to let her know not to make any mess or it won't be pretty for no one I wasn't accurately correct because she just keeps on creating new issues even if it didn't happen or hasn't happened yet she'll merely imagine an issue and try really hard to pin me as the monster that's fine because all lies and deception will be uncovered it's just a matter of time yes its bothersome to wait a long time and repeat the entire problem in your head and think why it's you in the middle but that's okay because I truly believe that what happened will uncover the truth and Uncle Harry will comeback to us but in the meantime I'll just have to wait patiently and see this through to the end.

Later on the week Uncle Harry had comeback from work and Lei had asked me if I wanted to go and get Uncle Harry from the garage where he leaves his truck. I told Lei yes I would go perhaps it'll give me some time alone to talk with Uncle Harry after we would drop off Lei at the house and go to Starbucks as he promised. What I mean by that is because when grandmother had argued with me and Uncle Harry heard

I just said that it isn't what it is and she didn't mean it. But Uncle Harry was very reluctant to believe it and said that when he comes back whatever I feel like I can tell him without feeling nobody is listening to me since I had some stuff to tell him. In truth it was just to tell him what Lei has been doing because as much as I wanted to tell him over the phone I couldn't she would always be around the corner listening into my conversations and making them seem like I was doing something wrong. I know I don't have a passcode on my phone but for Lei it seemed like an invitation for her to peep through my phone because I left it for 5 good minutes as I was heading for the bathroom and as soon as I leave and get back to my room I see that Lei has left the phone closed on WhatsApp now if anyone knows me I don't leave any tabs open so for me to see that I knew immediately that Lei has tempered with my phone for one grandmother doesn't know how to navigate a phone or even use it, quite a miracle she knows how to pick up calls otherwise she's unreachable. Reason two is that Lei is the only one who was present at the house to use a phone up to a 21st century born teenager standards she knows very well how to use a phone and for me to see that she has the nerve to pick up my phone and go through it amazed me quite badly. At this point I shouldn't really be shocked by Lei and what she does as she has shown me her true self on the first day. A little while after my grandmother yells for both of us to come and eat roll leaf rice which is a vegetable rolled with tiny pieces of meat and rice and it would be layed down in a pot side to the left and right but it would have meat just under the rolled rice leaf and if there is any rice leftover it would just be layed on top and covered with leaf for it to cook at a low temperature. I quite love this food and so does Lei because the first day we arrived to Detroit that's what she cooked for us, now if you're wondering how she knows I love this food is because before me and my grandmother left for Detroit Lei had called my mother to get a view on me personally but we didn't know what her true intentions were as she wanted to see what my mother says about me reflects to what Uncle Harry said which was false as she made the whole accusation up. My mother told Lei that I'm quite a picky eater which is true and everyone who knows me will know that I don't eat in the morning and will probably not eat anything after ate my lunch just because I'm not big on food however, if the food was already set on the table and asked to eat I will just because it is the proper thing to do and not to disappoint especially since Lei can talk harshly about me or more so spread lies to my mother. When grandmother called for us to eat I had assumed Lei would've been the first as she did mention she was super hungry and was waiting for the food to be prepared as she tried to get the food ready however, my grandmother doesn't like anyone to be in the kitchen with her unless they're by themselves and cook everything as well as cleaning because my grandmother hates the kitchen to be a mess which I totally understand. If the kitchen was to be a mess or not up to my grandmothers standard she would get up and go clean for as long as I remember my grandmother she just cleans and likes everything to be tidy even if there are guests she'd make sure the house is in the order which is what I admire the most about my grandmother. Although Lei wasn't at the table or even reply back to grandmother saying she isn't hungry or even reply back because Afterall grandmother is her mother in law she has to show respect instead Lei was packing her bags to leave how I know grandmother went to check in on Lei for the first time the door wasn't locked when Lei was in her room and grandmother yelled:

Why are you packing your bags?

Lei: Well your niece is driving me nuts and is going to divorce me between Uncle Harry and I don't wish to be near that energy?

Grandmother: She isn't going to be here anymore she's going to Uncle Williams house don't worry she's not going to be in your way no more

Me: I walk in and say what do you mean I'm going to Uncle William what did I do?

Lei: You deleted the photo!!!

Me: You didn't ask for permission otherwise I would've gladly shown you our conversation not that it's any of your concern.

Grandmother: You should've just shown Lei what she wanted she is older than you why not show her not like you're hiding anything??

Me: It's not about me hiding anything it's the fact that she took my possessions and did whatever she wanted without thinking of the consequences!

Lei: Why should there be any consequences I am your new sister so its fine.

Me: SISTER?!? My only sister is back in London you're nothing but a mere women that can be sent back to where she came from you're most definitely not my sister don't kid yourself!!!

Grandmother: It's okay if she calls herself your sister nothing wrong with it?

Lei: Yes, I just want to be close with you what did I say that was wrong?

Me: Everything you say is wrong and you don't even realise it which is just incredibly wrong!

Grandmother: I'm going to sit down I'm tired you two work out the issue and go out for coffee and have a nice time!

Me: My own thoughts (Out with her yeah right I'd much rather stare outside in the patio where the planes would go in and out of Detroit rather nice than being with Lei)

*Lei throws her clothes out of the suitcase and drags me by my hand *

Lei: What bothers you child?

Me: (In my thoughts) What child?

Lei: well talk to me...

Me: Nothing really I just didn't like what you did it's disrespectful to me!

Lei: I'm sorry I didn't mean to...

Lei proceeds to run off to grandmother and say we made up look she loves me again. I think that's a little dramatic we may be okay for now until her next plot to make me look bad or believe someone is trying to divorce her which I still find hilarious I'll let you know why. At a time I'm not quite sure when she actually mentioned that my grandmother is trying to divorce her. I find it quite hard to believe that as much as annoying this women (Lei) is, my grandmother loves Lei dearly I just don't understand my grandmother because she mentioned that Lei is annoying and doesn't wish to be around her as she's dirty and doesn't clean up after herself especially in her room which she mentioned to be atrocious. Surely if one was married they'd definitely care about their room but even if they hadn't married yet everyone cares about how their room would look especially since you wouldn't even want to be in it. Me personally I love my room to be tidy yes sometimes I can put off cleaning solely because I'm tired or just because I'm lazy but in the end I do straighten it up however, that wasn't the case with Lei when I entered her room for the first time let's just say what my grandmother said it did sound exactly how she described it to be. Lei's room was dirty I mean it had food scraps as well as some crunched crisp on the floor, clothes to be thrown from the closet to the floor and may I mention she has two closets so I do wonder what does she do in her room half the time if she doesn't clean up I mean surely if you're going to relax there you'd want to see a beautifully clean clear sight of the room. Her closets were extremely full so perhaps those clothes on the floor didn't fit in however she should just try to put them in one pile and figure out what to do with them rather than step on it but I guess she doesn't mind if we do. The only time Lei was ever productive in my mind was before I came to the USA and Lei was actually hanging up a chandelier in her room and I accidentally said I hope you fall but in truth I meant I hope you be careful I mean it just goes to show that this women is against good luck she just filled with bad luck I would never wish anyone to fall especially if you're doing something that requires you to be standing on a stool and hang, fix or apply but for it to splurge out of my mouth without me knowing truly shocked me and shortly after Lei said she fell perhaps she wanted me to feel guilty I'm not sure but it worked because it felt to me as if she fell purposely to tell Harry look what your niece said and I hadn't even met her yet. I wouldn't put it past her had she said that to Harry which does remind me when I arrived he did say do you remember what you said to Lei when you first spoke to her and said I hope you fall he started to laugh because he knows I would never say that I started to laugh too and Lei got super angry and was like oh look you have one brow why not separate them I mean the atmosphere completely shifted.

Harry: She never touches her brows they've always been one and besides it doesn't show.

Grandmother: Yes, she doesn't touch them and she looks absolutely beautiful with them!

Me: I don't particularly like to touch my brows just not something I'm comfortable with.

Lei: Well look at me I have two and I could totally take you to a salon and fix them only takes two minutes I promise!!!

Me: No thank you I don't wish anyone to touch them.

Lei: Sheesh I didn't know you were stubborn the lady at the salon will only pluck a few hairs!

Harry: Would you stop pestering the girl she said no leave it!!!

Me: (In my thoughts) Wow I didn't think she will tug on the few hairs it doesn't even show truly but hey maybe she just wanted me to have the same shape as hers? Who knows??

Grandmother: So what are we eating do you want me to get grilled chicken or perhaps see what we have and whip something up?

Me: (thoughts) Classic of my grandmother to switch the subject to food so like her to do that one of the qualities I love about her she knows how to switch an uncomfortable conversation to something I'm sure everyone loves FOOD!!!!

Lei: No mother in law it's okay I have cooked for us I'm sure you all will love I spent all day cooking it. I even asked your mother what you love so no excuse you won't eat.

Me: That sounded a little forceful but okay I will eat not much because we just had food on the plane.

Lei: Nonsense plane food doesn't fill you up its fake!

Me: What do you mean it's fake? It still is food I can assure you it's not fake at all and quite filling don't think I'll eat much but perhaps I'll have a proper meal tomorrow after all microwaved food tastes a whole lot better ha-ha!

Lei: NO THAT'S NOT FAIR I COOKED JUST FOR YOU AND NOW YOU'RE NOT GOING TO EAT A LOT!

Harry: Relax don't yell in the car I'm driving! My niece isn't much of an eater she's a big girl she'll eat when she wants to don't pressure her to eat. Besides you still have me and mother will eat with you after all I'm starving!

Lei: Yes I understand that but I cooked for her.

Me: I'll eat a little bit okay? Happy???

Lei: Wonderful of course I'm happy!

Me: (Thoughts) I guess this holiday will be one heck of a bumpy road better be careful if she got angry over food what else will tick her huh.

Harry: Okay we arrived go prepare everything I'll be back!

Everyone starts to leave I open and shut the door and Uncle Harry drives off and I slowly move myself from back seat to front Harry says what are you still doing here ha-ha I thought you left I said not at all I wish to spend some time with you after all that is why I came here now didn't I.

Harry: Why yes of course but aren't you tired you just came off a long flight wouldn't you want to go lay down?

Me: It's not like I'm running around now ha-ha I'm sitting here with you and having a blast!

Harry: Do you want coffee?

Me: Is that even a question of course I want!!!

Harry: Tim Hortons or Starbucks?

Me: We have a long month let's go to the nearest one and then go to Tim Horton tomorrow!

Harry: Sounds like a plan! Also I tried your recommended drink caramel macchiato it's actually quite good not very sweet you do indeed know your coffee.

Me: Of course I wish for you to try what I have everyday.

Me and Harry try and do everything together since I was a little girl he was someone I can tell everything and not worry about a thing he was like my best friend in the entire world. When my parents tell me and my siblings that we are going to Detroit for the summer I would be overjoyed knowing that I'll see my family but most of all Harry would be there and who knows what kind of fun activities we would do and the parks he takes us to or like no other we've been to before. Back in 2016 me and my older brother went to Detroit to see the family and unwind before school started which I wasn't looking forward to but the summer it was perfect. Harry and I had this competition to see who could grow their hair longer and he actually managed to grow it pretty long however it was extremely curly so when we'd extend the hair it'll go pretty far I think his hair went to his back which was impressive my hair was a tiny bit longer hence I won the competition and so my prize was anything I wanted. When you wage a competition and the prize is absolutely anything you kind of push to do anything to win the competition right I mean that's what I did, and so I asked Harry the real reason why he wouldn't marry anyone and he's like well I don't wish to be linked to anyone which got me thinking why think like that wouldn't you want someone to take pressure off you and help you around the house your someone who you can tell anything to your own best friend. He said well I just don't like the idea of marriage the amount of them just get destroyed with one or the other not communicating or them cheating on one another and I just don't have it in me to be hurt again which I understood and closed the topic down and asked if he wanted to grab coffee he didn't seem to be upset or hurt by the topic but from his voice it seemed like a very uncomfortable conversation and that's the last thing I wanted Harry to feel like. After we got our coffee Harry said I wasn't annoyed you asked that and could ask me anything you wanted so I jokingly said well okay lets continue the conversation but didn't really just wanted to see his reaction. But after Uncle Harry assuring me I can tell or ask him anything that's what I tattooed in my mind and never forgot that until he did marry Lei which was quite horrible for all of us especially on me since it's been cutting me up since 2022 and for all those sleepless nights I would cry myself to bed and when my friends ask me if I was okay I would lie and say yes even though it was wrong of me because I would fess up later and they would think why didn't I tell them earlier well because I'm the type to bottle my feelings up and make sure it never shows especially to those who I love the most and consider them to be my light for the day I just hope that this light I have doesn't fade away and for them to know they're appreciated. My time after coming back from Detroit was quite gloomy I didn't feel like myself for a very long time I would just hide the fact I was upset and empty inside I didn't want anyone to see the real me because I genuinely wasn't ready to let anybody in. To personally I felt nobody would understand me and that they'd think my issue was petty anytime I wanted to bring somebody in I was super scared of what they'll think and may just call it ridiculous. So what I did to keep myself occupied within the day time was to find any job didn't matter which one just that I had something to keep me busy from morning till late evenings and I was offered a job as barista which was very interesting to me because I love coffee and what's a better way than a coffee shop. But I will admit at times I felt more empty than ever and I didn't understand why I thought once I worked and kept myself busy I may start to forget about the situation but it turns out I felt more horrible at my breaks I would go sit on the stairs that would lead to the supply closet but one person knew but never told me why I was upset but always came to me and said If I was okay I wanted to ask why but it could come across as rude so I kept quiet and just answered with yes. One day my manager the one who asked me constantly if I was okay why do you sit on the stairs and not eat or drink anything or relax on your breaks I tell her I just want to be alone and sit where no one can see me she replied with I know why you sit there I can see you on the cameras my heart dropped even though I know I didn't do anything wrong it still surprised me that I wasn't careful that there was a camera and I didn't notice I was quite foolish only that my manager hugged me and said whatever is making you cry that badly and making you feel cold, empty and distant just know it's not worth your tears and you should think about the positive outcomes that are coming in your life. After hearing her nice words I couldn't help it but cry because Harry and grandmother words lingered in my brain as much as I wanted to forget about it I can't help but hear their words constantly it just felt like what they said was tattooed in my brain and to a certain point I actually believed what they said as if I was this horrible bad daughter who brings only shame to my family. But my manager assured me that even though I haven't known you for long you're definitely not what they said and that you're the best worker I've seen even if you haven't worked in a café before it felt very nice to hear pleasant words about me felt as if I haven't received anything good in my entire life because that's exactly how Harry made me feel. After my manager asking me to come into her office for breaks and not the stairwell seemed like I was wanted after feeling for an entire month I wasn't wanted and should be isolated made it seem like I was the worst company ever and this horrible girl who no one can stand if my own family didn't want me who else would it was a time where life struck me that I had to depend on myself and no one not even my own family would stand by me and if I wanted to achieve anything it was up to me to do it. When I arrived in Detroit I was feeling extremely happy about how the year would end but after leaving all I wanted was to not exist I wished and wondered about my life because the people I was with have well had loved me for 2 decades I just don't see anyone throwing that away for simply a new women just didn't make sense to me at all. They made my life my existence like a mistake as if they were forced to love me and put on a happy face for me since my mother was around but since it was only me there this time they took the chance to show me their true colours and it was to completely destroy me from the inside. The family I once loved and would do anything for made me rethink my future and I just cannot seem to step into Detroit anymore seems like a shut off place for me even though they don't control who comes and goes from Detroit but I just physically can't go there anymore this may sound silly but they were my soul purpose for Detroit my only reason to go there with no family to care or love for or even want me there what's the point of booking a plane ride and sitting idly on a uncomfortable chair for people who simply wish me out of the states why go? One of the reasons why I went along with my grandmother was because we didn't get the privilege to go to Harry wedding yes when I say privilege we didn't get the chance we weren't even thought of and Harry to marry and we were the last ones to know but everyone else knew it was quite hurtful to know that the man who I considered as my second father didn't even wish us at his wedding the one thing that only has a purpose once yes you may marry again and again but it's never as special and meaningful as the first. But after I had congratulated him I asked him why did you do it super early and not give us a chance to book a plane ride and prepare ourselves to come to your wedding he replied with well Lei was very anxious to get married and didn't want to waste anytime. I wasn't satisfied with Uncle Harry response but what was done was finale I couldn't change anything not like I had a time machine to revert to the wedding invitation stage oh well all I thought about was on 21st June it was my time to hang out with Harry and make new memories before university started. That's why I went with grandmother because I also wanted to meet Lei and see my family as it's been a while and they hadn't come to London so I thought I'd make the time and visit them. When you love someone a lot you'd do anything to see them and my family in the states meant the world to me I can't say for the moment I am quite angry and upset with them but deep down I still love them and if Harry came to me right this moment and asked for my forgiveness I'll give it to him all I want is for him to comeback and for me and my family not to feel like we can't go to Detroit no more because of Lei. For years I didn't realise what I had and took it for granted what I mean by that is my family and both Harry and William for granted thinking they'll always be here for us and never leave our side for anybody but for some reason me and my siblings were never ecstatic for Harry and William to marry when we first found out William had gotten married we weren't too happy as he slipped from us more and more when the days would pass. I just never understood why Harry and William became super cold and distant to me and my siblings as if we did something wrong, had we did let's say for example couldn't they just speak with us rather than ignore us or so much as say only a few words when we express ourselves so deeply in the texts with such love and care only to get a vague text but because we love them so much the vague texts they send we love and become overjoyed. Within their hectic schedules they would send us texts or sometimes they would call us and we get so happy to hear from them and how their day is going and what they've been up to.

On 1st July is my mother's birthday however, I was in the

states for about a week since I departed from London and I always buy my mother a huge cake as well as gifts box of chocolate and flowers. But this year I wanted to make it extra special by getting her a pair of earrings and ring to show her that no matter how far I am you're never going to feel that the day you were born isn't ever going to be celebrated. Now you maybe wondering well don't you have siblings and a father to be celebrating your mother's birthday in your absence yes I do, but my family tends to rely on me to make my mother's day special by preparing everything as well as the gifts ha-ha. I add my siblings name to the gifts even though my mother knows deep down who they're from which in the end of the day it's a special day to commemorate her birth into this world. So at around the day 1st July I couldn't even sleep because of how excited I was to hear what my mother thought of the gifts and the cake if she liked it and it would've been 4:30am my time at Detroit and 9:30am UK time. All I wanted at the time was to hear my mother's voice it was a nice change from what I've been hearing in the house and around Lei. When my mother sent me a message saying thank you and showing me the gifts I got her as well as the delivery of the cake at the time I thought it was best to deliver the cake rather than get one of my family members to wake up early and buy the cake just was easier on everyone. I'm not sure how or where Lei was but for some reason I hear her talking louder than usual telling grandmother and Harry that she's going to throw a party for grandmother and Harry and pretend it's their birthday since I'm here and she doesn't want me missing out I mean it's not like it would've been the first time I would miss out on their birthday but that is why phones exist for that exact reason to call them and send them birthday wishes and for me to send gifts by post no reason for her to create this fake party especially after my great grandmother passed away no one was in a party mood whether it was real or not. My grandmother is torn already it would just be disrespecting her and to be frank I didn't really want to spend anytime with Lei as I was forced to go out with her and buy party supplies but this is where I put my foot down and said no I'm not going out with her I also lost my great grandmother I'm mourning her lose why should I go out and buy supplies it just didn't make sense and that's when I said oh Lei have you never lost anyone is that why you party when someone passes away she didn't say anything but looked at Harry in a very angry way as if he's going to be punished for me not going out with her and for saying what I did but its true I mean you don't go partying when the entire house hold is mourning someone we loved dearly and wish was with us at that moment rather than Lei honestly I would rather ANYONE than Lei. What I wanted and even dreamed to get was out of the question even if it was food that I wanted to eat. You see I love soup any sort of soup and Panera bread has one of the best tomato soups I've ever had with a slice of bread and the amazing strawberry mint lemonade it was absolutely divine and most of all it was very close to where my grandmother lives just a 30min walk or even drive there like 15mins it couldn't get any better than that but Lei wanted to eat outside half the time preferably at a restraint which she'll order a lot of food and never even manage to finish her plate which she'll proceed to eat from others which is totally fine obviously had you finished what you ordered and that is always a large potion that she cannot finish. I mean why order such a large meal alongside sides when you know yourself it is to be a lot of food and its such a waste I for one never order anything and just eat what's left over since I hate wasting food personally I never include myself as if I'm not a human being who many wish to order something else but that's just how it used to be with Lei and Harry they're the main deciders whilst I was some sort of slave or what I say is a garbage bin that consumed what was left over since Lei also hated packing away the food we don't finish and just leave it behind like why you paid for it and if you liked the food so much just bring it with you why leave it behind you know it'll go to waste its just a horrible thing to do especially since you're not paying for the food so have some conscious and think of your husband who is footing the bill and be a nice respectable lady pack the food and eat it later in the day or even tomorrow no biggie and besides microwaved food is really good in my opinion. If I wanted anything I had to fetch it myself quite normal however, Lei hated the fact that I would go out without asking for her permission she would quite literally call me and say why is your niece going outside alone in this dangerous world she can be kidnapped now that seems very reasonable for her to be worried about me but her intentions were anything but sincere she only wanted me to be with her so she can show to Harry and William and grandmother that Lei is a lovely lady who cares for younger children/ young adults and can prove she can be a great mother one day. I did give Lei a chance when we go outside and she didn't care for nothing told me go on your own and when you're done let me know and will go home so what's the point of asking me to go places far when you're quite literally just going to leave me alone I could just walk around the neighbourhood which is really nice area no point of driving for hours in a heat tin can with someone who would love to see me on the side of road be with her and then leave me sits idly in a cafeteria and will wait till you're done. I just asked her if we could go home since I don't wish to be in a shopping centre I have no use for it and don't need anything if I did everything is back in London after saying that to Lei I did regret it because she did drive for long to get here but if you're just going to leave me I shortly took back my regret after all you're the one who is moaning to my Uncle and grandmother that you aren't spending enough time with me and want to take me to places that are exotic and far one shopping centres aren't far and two I don't particularly love sitting in the car long with Lei of course. When I was younger me and my brother as well as Harry and William will go on the highway with no destination in mind and have loud radio music on and just drive it was calming and nice because one the people in the car genuinely loved each other and two nobody had any schemes in mind as opposed to Lei who only wanted to go out with me to show Harry that she's taking care of me which will backfire and he'll say well why didn't you take care of Lei didn't I specifically ask that of you since she is this poor lady who doesn't speak English and can get lost yes because someone who used to live in Seattle for 7 years will get lost and has her driver's licence and has been to Detroit before because someone like her will get lost it was just a big fat lie. No one ever stood up to Lei which is why she has the guts to pretty much step on you and lie make you feel bad not even bad my apologies she'll make your life a living hell and it sucks worse than being around her entire family. I'd much rather be in the military serving the country stay there for many years than ever be in the same presence as Lei. There was a week after the whole drama Lei created when she wanted to get a job but couldn't because all of the requirements ask that she at least speaks and understands English which she cannot even speak a few sentences much less work in retail or food chain restaurant to serve customers. It was merely a difficult task that was handed to me as if I was ordered by the king or queen to get Lei a job when she is the one who is meant to get a job herself if she wants to pick and choose but Harry said it doesn't matter where she works so long its 5-10 minutes away from the house and she has to work a minimum of 3hrs a week like all those requirements are crazy no place will ever offer a minimum of 3hrs a week it has to be at least 10hrs or a bit more the least hours I've ever done was 15hrs and that would be split on the weekend because I was a student at university but her she does nothing all day and just eats or spends a lot of money by the way isn't hers she doesn't work for nothing I suppose that's why Harry wanted her to get a job so she at least has some spending money but it still doesn't make sense as to why I have to find her a job and anytime I did and explained each job role she didn't like it and said why are you only finding me jobs that are hard no job is easy hence why you'll get training and taught on specific items to use them properly according to company policy. I showed her Panera Bread which is only a 10minutes drive from the house and it's such an easy going comfy job which I personally thought she'd do well and it's a convenient place for her to work at but she didn't want it as it would make her smell afterwards it was such a stupid thing of her to say since when she cooks she also smells and standing in front of the oven at least working in Panera Bread you'll be serving others and learning life long skills which she thought she had already and didn't need to learn from anybody who's younger than her. Lei also didn't want to work in Walmart as she said its below her I was very ashamed when she said that one your husband aka Harry works as a trucker so are you also thinking he's below you and she said well no that's because it's his own company why on earth would I think he is below me I think he is the best and hardworking man which I proceeded to say so are the workers at Walmart they work so hard to keep the shelves fully stocked and clean also they can learn so much and honestly so can you if you gave it a try. But Lei still turned me down anytime I mentioned anything that has labour which was an impossible task from Harry to find her a job she'll love without lifting a finger or moving any muscles at this rate I just wanted to give up but grandmother kept insisting to find her job and let her gain some income but when she married Harry she specifically said I'm not here to work or give birth I'm only here to take care of your grandmother so you don't children or work that's fine but she doesn't even do the one thing she promised to do by taking care of grandmother and it completely switched around on grandmother as it seemed that she is the one taking care of Lei and organising the house as well as the plants and vegetables Lei planted and doesn't attend to their needs. Sometimes I think to myself how on earth did Harry marry such a selfish lady when all his previous women were such lovely ladies and had my grandmothers best interest at heart and wanted to even help you gain income help around the house and buy one that your grandmother loves and then you go marry a selfish lady. Lei asked me to teach her English and anytime I tried to give her reading materials she said I already read those and don't wish to read it again since my old teacher said reading the same book can get boring doesn't mean you don't have to read it again you can always reread the same book because you may have missed a few sentences or found a particular page very interesting and wish to read it again you can definitely benefit a lot from reading the same book I do to reread the same books also because I love to read myself.

When the incident happened where my relationship with Harry ended forever was on the 15th July 2022. He yelled at me and swore because I was nasty to Lei if I was truly nasty to her she wouldn't have gotten a MacBook and a job suited for her she quite literally doesn't even need to leave the house her job is remote all she does is lays down on the couch and work and half the time she makes me take over whilst she's locked in her room talking to her siblings. I done so many things to help them both out and yet it seemed like I was the problem. I do understand that maybe me and Lei didn't get off quite well at the start but I tried my absolute best to level with her it just felt like she hated me for some reason if I didn't comply to her requests which was to completely destroy my relationship with Beth and ignore William when he came over. Why?!? Why should I destroy the people I absolutely love in Detroit those who cared for me at my hardest times and guided me when I was younger from right and wrong, recommended me stuff that they know me and my siblings will love which surely was different to Lei when all she was interested was Harrys past and his dirty laundry nothing more nothing less she just had a different agenda to everybody else who just wished to enjoy each other's company she never even liked us which is why when anybody comes over she just walks out of the living room to her room and stays there comes out after the noise has died down and says well where did everybody go?!? I only wanted to change my clothes since my grandmother is gullible she'll believe anything mostly because she doesn't wish to cause any problems but the least she could've done was say well Lei you could've stayed in your previous clothing nothing was wrong with it and besides it is impolite to leave the room when guests have come over especially when they came for you. You should just stay for a little bit serve them tea and desert and ask them politely may I be excused and go do whatever you wanted. Shortly after Harry yelled at me I called my family back in London to hear what Harry is saying so I have proof had I not called them they wouldn't believe me because all my life Harry is this prime example of a good man someone you can rely on and now he completely changed 360 and wishes to cut his relationship with all of us and for what a women he met only 3 months ago who doesn't even love him and his mother but only wishes to gain connections and abuse him till he dried like a prune. My time back from Detroit was so hard that I had trouble sleeping and all I ever thought of was the issue I couldn't even go one day without crying and it wasn't just a simple sob it was more of a cry that would take all your energy make you drop to the floor and ask what on earth did you do to deserve such a horrid cry at 2am in the morning? I did my best to study hard to forget what happened which did work for a bit throughout the morning and evening but as soon as it was night everything was quiet my family went to bed and the house was quiet the only thing that was loud were my thoughts pouncing through my brain about what happened the more I thought about it I just felt like I was stabbed. I even got a part time job at a café because I love serving tea and coffee it would atleast bring me joy temporarily but when I was asked by my manager to take my break I would do anything to change it I didn't want my break because I knew the moment I sat down alone I would just think about the issue and the last thing I needed was to cry at work and feel all pathetic and weak.

Later that same night William comes to the house alongside his Beth and daughter to see me but I was so upset I just stayed in my room till William came to my room and said we come all the way here just to see you locked in your room at that moment it was just us I really did want to tell him everything but considering I know both Harry and William very well they'll fight right in the living room and that's the last thing I needed right now was another fight break out and let Lei think she has divided us which she has if I'm being completely honest. Before William he asked do you want to come with us without even thinking I said yes let me grab my luggage and went with them. I was so upset the last thing I wanted to do was stay in a house when people don't even like me and wish death on me by Lei of course she hates me so bad. William loaded by luggage and grandmother stood by the door crying I didn't really understand why she was crying as she played a part in the entire situation she was like a mother figure to me and quite literally said if there was anything you need come and talk with me and we can fix the issue together but anytime I spoke with her she completely shut me down and gave me the one finger silent sign as in don't talk and just watch what you see I was very confused what she meant by that why on earth shall I let this women hurt me when I'm here on holiday to see my loved ones and I ended up leaving Detroit with such unhappy ending and lost many people in the end and for what. William and Beth kept begging and pressuring me to tell them what's going on and if anything happened because I wasn't eating and looked like I was on the verge of dying as I looked pale and had bad under eyes after an hour of them asking I couldn't take it anymore since back at Harrys house they wouldn't even ask if I was okay so I just suppressed everything but when William asked me I just broke down in tears and told them everything they were so shocked they immediately called Harry and yelled at him and that's when things really went down hill because Harry claims he doesn't know anything about the problem and said well Lei claims that I was doing okay and eating and loved being with her and that Harry had proof of that when I was miserable with Lei. It felt like Lei had my entire life planned out and anytime they needed proof for anything Harry provided and it was all fake!

William: Asked does your mother know about this?

Me: No she doesn't!

William: Why haven't you told her anything?

Me: I didn't want to cause any problems besides grandmother said don't say anything you see only observe!

Beth: What do you mean only watch don't say anything?

Me: Well anytime I was on the phone with Harry when we were on good terms grandmother kept asking me you didn't tell him what Lei did to you today did you?!?

Me: I said no because you asked me not to and besides I'm not here for long so why should I cause problems it's his wife and he knows her not my problem.

William: I see! But you still should've told us when we asked you everyday when we came over!!!

Me: Well because minutes before you arrive to the house grandmother and Lei warned me about telling you guys anything and said you can look sad but not telling them anything. I wondered why as you're my family so there shouldn't be any issue if I told you what was going on or at least what's bothering me!

Grandmother insisted I shouldn't say anything to you both and if I did, she'll never talk to me again and put me on the next flight out to London. I mean I was the one who paid for the ticket not her and she can't even read or talk in English how else would she book me a ticket if her threat was real. Then she said Well Lei will book you the ticket she herself can't book me the ticket it was a joke that I can't even laugh at but laugh in my head at the ridiculous situation I'm in. William is furious with everyone especially at his mother for keeping me in the dark and in so much pain that he called my mother and spoke about this and then called my grandmother and was like our niece is the liar and she hurt Lei. Which Beth said I've known you (as in me) for 7yrs and not once has I lied about anything or caused problems and the issues only began when Lei entered the family. Beth just couldn't understand why Lei came with such hatred for everybody that she's met and hasn't it just didn't mellow in her brain hence the multiple questioning and repeat of the story. I kept explaining and told Beth and William exactly what happened they just couldn't believe Harry would do such a thing to me or grandmother as he said before I was even there his siblings and nephews and nieces are a red line not to be touched or said anything to the point where Harry was so fed up with Lei he wished to shove her out of the car. When grandmother came to William and Beth house she was so angry with me that she couldn't look me in the eye but after I told her what happened she was so shocked and embarrassed she still didn't look me in the eye but said please forgive me and started to cry because Harry loved us so much he couldn't possibly do anything to hurt us physically or verbally that's why it has us all very confused but anytime we tried to tell him what happened he wouldn't believe us he would mostly just yell at us and say NO THAT'S MY WIFE I KNOW HER WELL she wouldn't do what she did or what we claimed that Lei would do. After I came back to London I overheard the call between my mother and grandmother talking about how grandmother is doubting me and said well are you sure your daughter is telling the truth? Which made my mother say before she even went back to the states with you yourself complained about Lei how she's very dirty, not helping around the house, is incredibly rude and is two faced but when my daughter said something about your precious Lei it's not her fault and totally on my daughter just doesn't make any sense.

To be continued…

I would just like to take a moment to appreciate all the people in my life but one specific person I'll always be super grateful to they know who they are. Since the day I met them till now they have done nothing but support me every step of the way always there to cheer me up. May be miles away but it feels like they are here right next to me it's the kind of bond you will cherish forever.

Printed in the United States
by Baker & Taylor Publisher Services